CATSTRAWE

HELEN MAY WILLIAMS

Published by Cinnamon Press
Meirion House
Tanygrisiau
Blaenau Ffestiniog
Gwynedd, LL41 3SU
www.cinnamonpress.com

The right of Helen May Williams to be identified as author of this work has been asserted by her in accordance with the Copyright, Designs and Patent Act, 1988. Copyright © 2019 Helen May Williams.
ISBN: 978-1-78864-044-2

British Library Cataloguing in Publication Data. A CIP record for this book can be obtained from the British Library.
All rights reserved. No part of this publication may be reproduced, stored in a retrieval system, or transmitted in any form or by any means, electronic, mechanical, photocopying, recording or otherwise without the prior written permission of the publishers. This book may not be lent, hired out, resold or otherwise disposed of by way of trade in any form of binding or cover other than that in which it is published, without the prior consent of the publishers.

Designed and typeset in Palatino by Cinnamon Press. Printed in Poland.

Cover design by Adam Craig © Adam Craig.

Cinnamon Press is represented in the UK by Inpress Ltd and in Wales by the Welsh Books Council.

Acknowledgements

Some of these poems or parts of them have been published, often in previous versions, in the following publications: *Slim Volume: This Body I Live In*; *Ink Sweat and Tears*; *Haiku Journal*; *The Interpreter's House*; *I am not a silent poet*; *Envoi*; *The Iafor Vladimir Devidé Haiku Award* (2016); *Allegro*; *Paper Swans*; *the curly mind*; *Three Drops from a Cauldron: Samhain 2015, A Poem to Inspire*. My thanks to all those editors for finding merit in my work.

My cousin, Lesley Allwood-Coppin (née Dennis) has been actively engaged in researching our Dennis family history. I am grateful to her for sharing her finds, especially material relating to Catstrawe in St Clether, Cornwall.

I am deeply indebted to Jan Fortune, whose encouraging but disciplined mentoring assisted me in transforming a plethora of haiku and tanka into a finely-honed collection.

Finally, none of this would have been possible without the constant support of my husband, Ian Williams.

Helen May Williams lives in South West Wales, where she regularly leads poetry workshops. Her poetry sequence, *The Princess of Vix*, was published by Three Drops Press in 2017. As Helen May Dennis, she formerly taught at the University of Warwick and published on twentieth-century North American literature and poetry. She blogs at:
helenmaywilliams.wordpress.com

Contents

Mid-winter	9
Cancer Diary 1	11
Lent in Provence Vert 1	13
Cancer Diary 2	16
Lent in Provence Verte 2	17
Easter 2015	19
Doing Probate	22
Cancer Diary 3	25
pondering the various kinds of oppression...	27
Funereal Reflections	29
Catstrawe	30
I start the month of July with more anxiety dreams	34
Cancer Diary 4	36
at Dylan's Shed	38
on hearing Gareth Williams' Fields of Light	40
Sousse Massacre	41
Light Haiku 1	42
leaving Anywhere	49
Kraków Cityscape	52
Light Haiku 2	58
drest in his surplice in Eglyscimmon church-yard	61
Now	62
chance encounter above Zacopane	66
Bataclan Paris	68
on March 22nd Bruxelles terror attack	71
Hag Haiku	72
Endnotes	74

for my sons Aaron Dennis and Alex Dennis
my daughter Georgie Dennis-Guise
my grandchildren Abigail, Ethan and Rose

my son asks   how can
you say you're busy
you no longer sell your time

how can I tell him
his hour-glass is full —
I watch each hour sift away

Catstrawe

Mid-winter

> 1 January - 6 January
> for my mother, my daughter, & my granddaughter

I prepared chestnut stuffing
for the first time
fifty years ago

a child determined
to prove herself a better
cook than you, mother

you slipped unawares
into waking dawn bearing
lost memories with you

young, she tugged my apron strings
now she tugs my heart
soon she will give birth

deep curve of the bay
wind sweeps breaking waves
Hebe blooms impervious

live in the here and now
sit in expectant stillness
hear resounding silence

her labour begins
I sip camomile
knit in expectant silence . . .

      text message received 6 January 01.05
as of 22.50 you have a
beautiful 6lb 14 oz granddaughter
It was all very quick and everyone is very healthy

green spirits sheltered
twelve days — now
turf them out

rough grass : golden fleck
male blue tit alights
ritual feast for spring plumage

Cancer Diary 1

      03 January   the cancer specialist is interviewed
all cancer is luck
or bad luck he says
an opportune way to die

      05 January   on Dennis Potter
now he sipped morphine
knew his own death   saw
the *blossomiest* blossom

      16 January   The du Maurier filter tip is cool and clean with a fine satisfying flavour. And the smart gold-embossed red box keeps the last cigarette as fresh as the first. You'll enjoy everything about du Maurier.
while pregnant with me
still Mummy sported their
ubiquitous red & gold

'just say, I love you,
yawn, light a cigarette
and walk away.'

      28 January   *Nox pars obscura diei est* —
      and I get simple Welsh greeting wrong!
already I drop
syllables   switch suffixes
mouth weird confusion
Babel of stark tongues: night ... nacht...
nuit ... noce ... notte ... nos~~waith~~ ...

Sunday, 01 March   on hearing Maurice Chevalier on *France
Musique* and recalling my mother's mastectomy
when I was eight years old

how did she feel
at the Radium Institute
an anxious patient
no longer an almoner
her body a battle-field . . .

12 March   for the past week almond trees have emerged into
bloom

gnarled old wayside tree
white blossom   Hades dark trunk
cleansed Provençal sky

Sunday, 22 March   at dawn

from the night's silence
each morning to carve one thought
or excavate many

30 April   preparing for my next procedure in Glangwili Ysbyty

in early faint light
five sheep asleep by the gate
I wake at five

14 May   mourning my daughter-in-law's mother, Bernie Malpas
29/01/1957 to 14/05/2015

be they ever so
difficult   once we lose them
we miss them   always

Lent in Provence Vert 1

> 02 March the past is senseless
> Jorie Graham

for Lent we eschew
internet hot baths Today
serious news — why?

> In the month before he died, my father Harold Noel Dennis
> described himself as 'restless for all these years.'

... also gardening
watching daffodils push through —
restless like Denny

> 03 March

dusky black redstart
unfurls rust-ochre plumage
tail feathers catch fire

he flies fans alights
on pollarded branch then flits —
solitary show-off —
to *pelouse anglaise* to catch
emergent cicada

> 04 March

Lent: no radio
no portal to current events
no fast betterment

the word I write most —
check: check dates   check facts   check names —
past slips through my grasp

    Thursday, 05 March
ninety-three today
happy birthday to you, June —
ash heap in sand dune

her favourite tune
Non, je ne regrette rien —
of course it's not true

from the age of five
she always slipped the first stitch
at the start of each row
I chose not to copy her —
I use her needles today

my hair style's not mine
the shape of my face has morphed
I am my mother

check spelling — again
June's spelling was always fine
much better than mine

Rose is three months old
I knit her next year's sweater
& watch black redstart —
his rosy-tailed prolepsis
of evening's salmon skies

clear night sky — full moon . . .
un ciel clair — une pleine lune
cinq heures — la boulangerie
allume le rond-point

I've passed moon-lit night
French monologue in my head
illuming nothing

        06 March *Phildar aiguillles circulaires*
        longueur 100cm diamètre 3 ¼ –
I knit onto these —
bought when: in forties Paris?
to reknit what wool?
ECITO *après la guerre*
stitched an unravelled Europe

        07 March
chic insouciance
of *provençal printemps* &
of the ginger cat
lolling on red-tiled wall
waiting for lone black redtail . . .

Cancer Diary 2

    07 April   Glangwili Ysbyty
roseate lichen
mossy tufts on smooth wall —
bladder cancer

    08 April   last night's dream
mouse crouches in bin —
Chernobyl cafe waitress
pink flesh   brittle bones

    20 April   05:54 greeting the sunrise over Eglwys Gymyn
that morning will come —
no longer to salute you
rosy-fingered dawn

    22 April   witnessing the false dawn
early morning view
where lawn mower cut too deep —
sliced off crocus leaves

    Sunday, 10 May   witnessing the sunrise
when the mind falls numb —
sow coriander heartsease
pale forget-me-not

Lent in Provence Verte 2

> 12 March   and for the past week
> almond trees have emerged into bloom

lichened trunk by school fence
pink blush grimes urban white
last year's nuts still cling

> 18 March   *dans un gîte barjolais le soleil est de retour*

the sun has returned
metallic pink flamingo
stands sentinel

our hosts have cut canes
on the road towards Correns
their tomatoes will grow tall

old-man tree blooms first
profusion of foam
against a spring-cleaned sky

old man tree sprints into spring
our camera dawdles — snaps
faded blossom emergent leaves

> Sunday, 22 March   *en regardant les gravures anciennes
> pendues aux murs de notre chambre*

red is first to fade
then yellow   then green —
cærulean remains

      23 March   on Pierre Bonnard

first task each morning —
gather the day's provisions
stroll to his atelier

mount narrow staircase
place his harvest
of ephemera —
gleaming leaves blowsy blossom
sunlight through trees

      on Pierre Bonnard's last painting of an almond tree

hibernal petals
celestial blue advances
dead branches recede

      after Louis-Ferdinand Céline

memories are young once . . .
turn into rotten ghosts —
apples left to spoil

Easter 2015

      06 April   on my father's birthday
shrivelled casement
last year's dahlia rhizome
carefully labelled

        I recall when I was the age my eldest granddaughter is now
pom pom flower-heads
a child lost in their foliage —
sub-urban harvest

      08 April   22:01
clear night sky   bright moon
mouse-hole exposed in border
cat paw tracks on soil

      10 April   on witnessing a selfie at Barafundle Bay
clouds drift on sky's swell
spumed surfer scales cliff   assembles
seascape with surfboard

      on witnessing fatherhood
dad risks life & limb
rescues plastic orange ball
from yellow gorse

       with my eight-year old granddaughter
       and her seven-year old brother

tourists tramp headland
kids skit over scurvy grass
lark sings to distraction

       11 April   on finding the eleventh best way to amuse grandchildren

(N)arbeth castle mound
Rhiannon at its gate —
Epona erased

Flemish chimneys   their
phallic stacks espoused stone once —
lost palimpsests

neighbouring homes
purloined their DNA
gone the usual way

       Sunday, 12 April   late evening with my son and daughter-in-law

at the kitchen table
we consider the future —
my grandchildren sleep

selfish genes survive
selfish designs decay
kids play their own way

13 April   family holiday with grandma
children sleep wake play
children sleep again till eight
children wake play go

15 April   remembering my father's garden
hybrid T rose-bed
south-facing dahlia border
dank air-raid shelter

tall trees   formal lawn
Spanish hyacinths   Dutch elms
cinder woodland path

who is left to remember
his days spent clearing ivy?

Doing Probate

   14 April 22:43 recalling this morning's trip to the recycling facility
her Roberts radio
goes for recycling at last
another link lost

as I drive away
a waste disposal worker
picks it from the bin
my mother's old radio
reprieved

   17 April our neighbour reminisces
too many helpers came
to clean village hall roof
so he used his machete
to clear Japanese knot weed —
just like in Burma

how many were there
came back and never (n)ever
mentioned it again

   18 April remembering my mother's one attempt
   to help my father gardening
one slice with the hoe —
they lie severed uprooted
the pansies he sowed

13 April   23:27
hill-top sea mist
young badger in headlights
clambers back up bank
he seems too small
compared with previous road kill

26 April   late afternoon
the great tit is dead
his body lies perfected
stiff yellow & black
right claw lifted & curled
no match for the strong north wind

27 April   early morning
predators retire
cock great tit still lying there —
an overlooked feast

28 April   03.15 having planted snake-bark maple trees
with my husband that afternoon
the wheelbarrow's lost
we search the garden —
it stands beside us
while we open garage doors
& peer in every corner

they're not keeping up
these minds   that think themselves young
miss the obvious

death is always there
we look around it   through it —
fail to see it

      29 April
then the tit was gone
no plumage left lying
buzzard   fox   kite   young cat?
in our neighbourhood   reside
enough wild undertakers

I walk the garden
inspect native bluebells
yellow rattle   lady's smock —
from the old ash tree nest-box
great tit chicks cheeping

Cancer Diary 3

    20 May   10:54 the crazy logic of my dreamscape lingers
    to mid-morning

the brown bowl is cracked
crazed down its left side —
I unpack my life

next in my luggage —
the delicate cardigan
unravels before my eyes

so we pitch our tent
on the hilltop — views for miles —
not in the teeming maze of
out-lets sit-ins take-aways

alongside us
a pale-blue Ford popular
with three passengers —
as we pitch our old green tent
two women lean in to kiss

awake I realise
that was my mother's first car —
but whose was the kiss?

    23 May   pondering a conversation with the artist Andrea Kelland

meeting each deadline
snapshots of my life —
& that final deadline waits

      26 May   06:00 anxiety dream on waking

dark deep concave pit
witness friable walls crumble —
pitch in & fill it

      06:59   hope prevails over mug of green tea

my aquilegia
great-great-grandchildren
of those Denny grew
two mutations have emerged:
deepest rose & darkest purple

      04 June   at the histology clinic

those pretty pink tufts
we excised & cauterised —
mere inflammation

pondering the various kinds of oppression in the world and realising that none of us are entirely innocent

       16 June   careless gardening

robin twitters at barn's mouth
as I go to take pebbles
from under the pile
of disused bulk bags —
I don't see the nest

we twitch a corner
& there they nestle in a crease
pale precarious eggs

       17 June   Ventimiglia: in this Italian border town situated roughly 10 kilometres east of Menton, France, hundreds of migrants have been stranded on the rocks lining the coast for several days now.

'meandered around this
charming old town
perfect to stay in
for Monte Carlo Grand Prix
at Monaco —

'just a gentle
thirty-minute train ride
down the Riviera'

'lovely little bars
hand sewing machines . . . fake bags
hawkers' fragile tack
police should really clamp down'
'beautiful old Italian town'

six days on the rocks
six cases of scabies —
police remove with force

    18 June

tattered histories
ripped-up   reduced to rubble /
frayed   shattered   futures

the precariat
clings to lampposts ducks truncheons —
hands protect heads

that's the fourth summer
we've disturbed the robins' nest —
they still confide in us
flit in under my spade
for the juiciest worms

    19 June   *Laudato si', mi' Signore*

the Earth our home
an immense pile of filth —
she cries out to us
we forget we too are dust
our bodies her elements

    June 20 on the discovery of a mafia illegal waste disposal site
    60 km from Naples

with shovels we found
that the soil was blue or pink —
beneath the surface

Funereal Reflections

>02 July   in memoriam Reverend Keith Littler
>vicar of Eglwys Gymyn Church 1994 -2004

I have placed flowers
white lilies   gladioli
iris   marigold —

I could say *for the repose of your soul*
but I know I placed them
for the repose of ours

>03 July

naked we arrive
we stay awhile   that's it
naked we depart —
who wouldn't want a soul to
console them on their visit

>it is sown a natural body; it is raised a spiritual body.
>1 Corinthians 15

a spiritual body
magic by analogy
a transient thought

swallow chicks clamour
by *yn afon Calfari*
from precarious porch nest

nor Denny nor June
wanted monument
nor tombstone

Catstrawe

> Sunday, 05 July   History is something that very few people have been doing while everyone else was ploughing fields and carrying water buckets.
>
> Yuval Noah Harari

John Dennis — Ashwater
George Dennis — Egloskerry
Thomas Dennis — St Clether
Nicholas Dennis — Altarnon
John Dennys — St Clether

      15 July

Year — 1664
Hundred — Lesnewth
Parish — St Clether

John TREVILLIAN
Esq. in Catstrawe in which
lives John Dennis a poor man —
New Taxpayer Forename — John
New Taxpayer Surname — Dennis

Notes: Hearth Tax, Cornwall —
Hearths not mentioned
in the former returns

he was 'a poor man'
my seventh great grandfather —
hearth taxed nonetheless

— which begs the question
what on earth & where on earth
was Catstrawe?

      16 July
camera eye sees
records directly   but now
we copy / paste &
copy / paste to power of ten
read digital palimpsests —

our world washed ghost white
hand-me-down knowledge shimmers
makes intricate moves
through paragraphs of data
shimmy-shakes on restless screens

'we want to know stuff
we're human   we explore'
utters cyber-voice

> 18 July   On a journey north, we visit my mother's cousin. He is the closest connection to my mother now. We arrive too early and pass the time before ringing his doorbell by walking on Ainsdale strand. Each childhood summer my father sculpted Noddy's car from damp sand here. All the splendid beach houses whose facades face out to sea are long-since derelict.

vacant beach houses
red bricks gleam in July sun
boarded windows stare

My parents' wedding was sixty-six years ago this summer. They lived here all their married life. Neither came from here originally. All that remains of them now is a small tin plaque on a sea-sprayed board that says they donated to the pier restoration, and a dwindling heap of mingled ashes in a hollow on their sand dune.

ceaseless swallows swoop
shelter under exposed beams
toy with onshore breeze

20 July   We stay at Weldale House, where my mother panic-bought a flat after my father died. Here she struggled to make a solitary life after half a century of marriage.

one fake yellow rose
sentinel in this strange place
death's watch-tower

21 July   Having driven north to Applecross, we pitch our tent in the late evening; too late to discover that we forgot to pack its inner shell. As dusk falls, we sleep in the musty shelter of an abandoned tent. All around us brawny men prepare for tomorrow's Highland Games. One of them leaves the wooden gate ajar as he returns from the pub in the village below.

crepuscular light
roe deer munch grass
through the snores

Sunday, 26 July

Monday was Tyndrum
then Tuesday thru Friday was
Applecross — view spanned
Sound of Raasey to Skye & —
Black Cuillin & Red Cuillin

bound to standing stone
dark Cúchulainn was vanquished
we'll forget of course
quaff time's potion   erase sights
sounds   all emotions — quench lights

> 27 July   I have checked for the name of Catstrawe on the tithe map system for St Clether circa 1840 to see if it is a tenement name but found no entry. I have also looked in books of Cornish place names and our online historic mapping system but unfortunately to no avail.   It is possible that the name has got corrupted over time, spellings often change through the ages and sometimes disappear altogether. I am sorry we cannot find a conclusion to this enquiry. Yours sincerely, The Archivist.   Archives and Cornish Studies Service, Cornwall Record Office, Cornwall Council.

spellings often change
disappear altogether —
just like DNA
names corrupted over time —
just like Cúchulainn → Cuillin

> Postscript 16 October

catstrawe = a herb
but now the manor is named
Basil Farm instead

> Post Postscript 21 October   Michael Westcott, St. Cuthbert's Place, Wells, Somerset, Sept 13th, 1852.

'. . . part of an oat-straw
with the joints cut off
. . . that I gathered in a wood called Clethe,
on Cornish side of Tamar' —
Oat straw not Catstrawe perchance

I start the month of July with more anxiety dreams

    01 July

boss gone raving mad
her employees cluster   cluck —
lost distraught chickens

customers creep out
yet encounter her stark gaze
her un-made visage

racks of picture cards
form a body-guard   surround
her primordial screech
god gone raving mad stalks
cathedral gift shop

    06 July   00.01

what a time to wake
to catch one day as it turns
into the next one

death stands at bus stop
beneath his feodora
his cool eyes watch us
crushed head on floor boards oozes . . .
we survey the scene and leave

life-in-death leans out
upstairs window   spits venom
barely misses me
we cross over   walk on by
glad to be alive — still

every step we take
we lurch against gravity —
walking miracles

       10 July   dawn between waking and waking
walking there we crossed
the edge of a loch   keeping
our goal in sight — till

we veered a half circle
unnerved   started to tramp back
but the path was gone
its trace submerged   in its place
an enchanted silver sheen

we would have turned back
to shelter in the lobby
but stayed staring at
this remote highland landscape
pondering our journey's end

Cancer Diary 4

    Sunday 11 January   Who owns the narrative of my life? Do I own my own story? Do I own my children's? Or are these stories just brief gasps in the flow of time, to be submerged in anonymous rememories?

nurse's quiet word
starving myself to death
will keep me alive

    Sunday, 01 March
    on hearing Maurice Chevalier on *France Musique*

singing in the rain
I rehearsed that for Brownies
then June got cancer

Denny drove me down
Saturday
    drove back Sunday
giving up his week-end

he stayed just long enough
for early-morning walk
his best shoes mired in cow-pat

our adventure — just
Denny & me playing hookey
not sensing their fear

       14 March   *I've sown cerinthe seed* — message from my daughter
in their tiny pots
will the cerinthe I sowed
survive the March gales?
I inherited those pots
from Denny along with anxiety

       Sunday, 24 May   recollecting yesterday's walk along the River Teifi
air full of white down
trees assume a festive look —
fluff-seeds drift off crack willow
I trample sallow-snow
& wych elm's scattered seed

at Dylan's Shed

>19 September - 21 September
>for Mab Jones

Tâf cliff-top garden
breeze snags her washing
badgers snuffle apples

capsized snail sways
on spiral keel atop fencepost
tumbles into brambles — safe

heron's descendent
still priests Tâf's estuary
stands solitary in sand
— but for seagull altar-boy

silent liturgist
shoreline's sole officiant
— while poets prattle

whole families
tear up their passports
buy Syrian fakes
escape through cornfields

shall I say
I would wait my turn
in camps turned jails
among the wretched of the earth?

badgers & rats
pilfer sweet apples — foxes
& seagulls watch

across the Tâf: *church*
the size of a snail protrudes
its horns — not *through mist*:
the day is clear dry bright and
illumines broad *sea wet* sands

on hearing Gareth Williams' *Fields of Light*

    22 October

father at kitchen window
sucking on pipe tobacco
rich dark honeydew

first up each morning
making breakfast tea
carefully placing
cups, saucers, rich tea biscuits —
one apple shared between two

father at kitchen window
washing the Sunday dishes
smoking Gallagher's
rich dark honeydew watching
blackbird robin & bluetit

always vigilant
to discourage the starlings —
Burmese nightmare vultures

forgetting to check
the dishes for leftover smears —
mother quietly re-washed

Sousse Massacre

      Sunday, 28 June
bathing in the sea
camels swayed along shoreline —
'very very calm' . . .

he was twenty-three
decent break-dancer —
strolling on sand   gun in hand

      29 June   10:29   a tangle of nightmares haunts me this morning
shredded pink scraps in
drawstring muslin bag —
intestines?   humanity?

Light Haiku 1

       Sunday 18 January
slight sliver of waning moon
hangs above etched trees
silver crescent on azure

three ravens flap by
dark silhouettes of willow
dawn glint on dewpond

       21 January
Lundy & Caldey
float on marine light
upturned coracle halos

       24 January
new moon waxes wakes
over flailed hedgerow —
shredded branches / broken limbs

03 February to 'Old Fool'

you go downstairs
in the middle of the night
to turn off the moon

04 February

late-afternoon sun
illuminates crocus trail
through snow-covered grass

21 February 06.00 *Samedi noir*

ferret? shrew? fox?
forêt d'orient pre-dawn . . .
glimpsed through reverie

24 February

mistral sweeps sky clean
sends folk scurrying indoors —
old fool sun bathes

        Friday, 20 March   10.00 —
          waiting for partial eclipse of the sun (80%)

high cloud from the north
I don dark glasses — in vain
no sight of the sun

       on seeing it mediated by BFM TV

cloud obscures the sun
then passes   now it's too bright —
we watch its screen image

this golden halo
this sense of expectancy
this sapphire stillness

for these few moments
the desert fathers prayed —
waited their whole lives

21 March *mon anniversaire / la grande marée du siècle*

joyous the year turns
new moon draws tides high on shore —
I draw breath sit quietly

24 March Pesco Luno thinks
he has fished the moon from
the River Argens

Stuff you, joker cloud!
My Mother Moon, have mercy!
I have fished and sinned . . .

any Friday night
gone fishing to catch moon-beams
reflecting on dreams

18 April
constellar patterns
Orion glimpsed through ash trees . . .
then pre-dawn glow

05 May
I watch the pink light
smudge the eastern horizon
dawn after dawn

18 May   20:32
shaft of evening sun
catches rabbit in mid field —
more composed than I tonight

03 June 22.45
shepherd moon drifts
over hazel blackthorn ash
watches ewes and lambs

full moon drifts softly
through my fretful sleep . . . eyes nose
pursed lips — Pierrot face

Venus / Jupiter
so bright they shine even
through photopic city lights

subjugated to
the same universal laws —
not law-givers after all

Saturday, 01 August   on day of blue moon at top of Pendine hill
brightness flows through air
Rose hears wind tousle ash trees
ruffle *Cupressus*
rustle windmill palms —
eyes wide open to hear

07 August   on getting lost in *Luckenwald*
to leave we drove east
following sunrise — old man
said follow that track

landstrasse byways
hayfields gold in morning light
joggers out early

ignored sign 'No Cars'
navigated by sunrise —
illicit exit

leaving Anywhere

      08 August – 30 September

learning Polish from
an USSR magenta text book
that tries to deny
existence of Polish speech
states it's a young language
a fly by night eruption
soon to be quelled

learning Polish from
an USSR magenta text book —
the only one I can find
anywhere in Poland —
twenty-seven years gone
repeating stock phrases
to get me through customs

learning to order tea & coffee
while I thump the iron
passing and repassing my sons'
shirt-cuffs, shirt-collars, shirt-fronts
and leave the sleeves to last
while I pack their lunches
tidy Lego from hearth rugs …

***

twenty-seven years gone &
entry to Poland bumpy
road so degraded
it's not called a motorway —
for kilometres we creep
over cracks pot-holes & past
collapsed carriageway

at least I'm not stopped
led to an airless room
questioned by weary police —
slouched over a rough-hewn desk
watched warily as my
stock of phrases fails me
as my tears creep down my cheeks

joined by his colleague
(she has rudimentary English)
pointing to my visa:
Where are your children? *At home*
my children wait at home —
I misunderstood visa
listed their names in error —
on the minuscule baffling form

***

now who needs a visa?
not us crossing an
unmanned border
in forty degrees of august heat
wondering where we'll find
the next cup of coffee or tea
to keep us alert & pert

none of the above
starts to touch terror
fear of unfamiliar —
not even *unheimlich* —
for first few alien days
leaving Anywhere
with no route back

Kraków Cityscape

    10 August   Polish radio advises the elderly to stay indoors
    between 11.00 & 16.00 during heatwave

young woman
sets takeaway
before silent hag

gnarled hands pull open bag
hooked nose sniffs
proffered food

her dark eyes glimpsed —
in afternoon's intense heat
she eats

    14 August
waste ground parched track
tall golden rod by tram
grass stalks turn straw

when our star tumbles
then corn-stalk calamity
haunts our dream byways

Saturday, 15 August   Assumption of the Blessed Virgin *Nowa Huta*

sweet-smelling bouquets
finest blossoms
green of healing herbs

clutched in hands
proffered for sale
citrus greens electric blues
folk art reds —
city streets ablaze

hushed light goldenrod robe
gilded stars on midnight blue
slight virgin sways to hold Him —
childlike gaze transfixed
she blesses these simples

in *Mogiła*'s Abbey
I knelt & wept before her —
breathed in the yellow roses

Sunday, 16 August   13:25

even in this flat
we cannot ignore
the absolute thunderstorm —

counting seconds between flash
& boom
watching pine tree top

as we ran for tram
down & outs disputed
or sketched their view of nature

how do the homeless
keep sketchpads dry —
find shelter from rain

17 August   anniversary of my parents' wedding day, 1949
(black sash & black hat
white dress & white heather
long dark page-boy curls

between church & reception —
in photographer's studio
my father stands to attention)

heatwave aftermath —
sirens screech all day
the milk in the fridge
turns to curds & whey
in-date salads fizz

a man lies prone
face placed in recovery
under an umbrella —

half a dozen umbrellas
stand around
in attendance

an ambulance nears
waiting for pedestrians
as they splash across

gutters spew old leaves
& birds-nest sticks —
spout grey waterfalls

      18 August I dream
changing Rose's nappy
she says her first words —
'fresh air' — needs fresh air . . .

      21 August from entry for '*The Plena*, annual, or double-flowered sensitive mimosa.' *Encyclopædia Britannica* 1797
spikes of yellow
pentandrous flowers
rise from unarmed stems

sensitive
to touch of air
anticipating autumn

but here is invasive
golden rod — not mimosa
displacing natives

yet the reed warbler
moves from stem to stem
unafraid — at home

> 22 August

I text my daughter
I dreamt her first words
'fresh air!'

my daughter texts back
I dreamt it was: 'No!'
'fresh air' / 'No!' — both could be right

> *szombat, augusztus 29*

aymonym [autoput]
autópálya
autobahn

Light Haiku 2

      20 August 21:09 Kraków
here the new moon shines
above rooms rented hourly —
onto corner shop

I buy rosé wine
kabanos 'camembert' cheese
walk home by moonlight

      Sunday, 23 August 19:15 after 9 hours driving
      on Polish and German motorways
not a holy day
although the sunset over
Chemnitz inspires awe

01 October

on rose-tinted wash
four vapour trails tracing *DAWN* —
sky's calligraphy

02 October   morning

primrose yellow sun
glacé-mint blue
late waking at eight

02 October   evening

driving past Cardiff
low moon sullen blood-red —
reach out and pluck

03 October   in Coventry

waking to cloud &
last week's clarity obscured —
mindful of the light

Sunday, 04 October   midday Coventry

October sunlight
drying my son's white work shirts
in his back garden

05 October   after Stephen Hawking

to understand lights
know about life, about minds —
shining from planet Earth

drest in his surplice in Eglyscimmon church-yard

>04 July   In the county of Carmarthen there is hardly one that dies but some person sees his light or candle, when the spirit is supposed to glide swiftly by.
>
>>from E. Spence. *Summer Excursions*. Volume II. 1809

moonlit night walk home —
beheld his own figure beside grave
reading burial service

a week afterward
performed burial service
on very same spot

saw a light approach —
'a death light' borne
by an invisible hand

Now

> 15 September & 17 September

now Turks-head pumpkins
trail across wet concrete
their fruits still tiny

> now there's a heatwave
> in Europe — even in a
> freezer truckload of
> so-called immigrants

now nasturtiums shed
their caper-substitute pods
before the first frost
wilts their peppery leaves

> now father & daughter
> cross so many borders
> walking for days through —
> serbian / croatian /
> hungarian / german

now borage stems break
with an excess of blue
star-like flowers still
harbouring anxious bees

       now she skips along track
       through gap in razor-wire fence
       carrying her teddy

now hardy orange
gold & yellow marigolds
continue to bud bloom
& set scimitar seeds

establishing their home
in this temperate Welsh plot
undeterred by westerly gales

       now rumours from ahead
       name it the death route / yet
       father and daughter
       still walk it — tear-gas /
       hunger / thirst / opprobrium

now verbena bay
rosemary thyme stay
in outdoor beds &
pray for a clement winter

       now in searing heat
       steel gates straddle carriageway
       razor-wire unfurls

now almond trees
shake in equinoctial breeze
yearning for the sharp
dry cold of the Pyrenees
only one generation away

        now tear gas canisters &
        water cannon bombardments
        target baby-carriers —
        young men hurl rocks back

now blight infects
outdoor tomatoes
(their name an indecipherable
smudge on greyed labels)
before their fruits can ripen

and courgette flowers
slime their soft mildewed rot
on immature fruits

        now is such a time
        of arid silenced prayer
        of forced bivouac
        on fenced-in alien
        hard-shoulder tarmac

now spring's ebullient sowing
is a few scattered notes
in an abandoned
blue gardening journal

       now babies are held out
       and toddlers crawl
       on no-man's land appealing
       to lines of frontier guards
       in riot gear

yet aquilegias
self-seed in neglected pots
and finally I have planted
home-grown bergamot

       while in Hungary's
       humane corridor
       human packages are
       delivered swiftly

chance encounter above Zacopane

   Sunday afternoon 5th June, 2016

1
'Poland is pink now.' he said
   but meant to say 'pretty'
      piękny as a picture
    & the fine palette of transformative grammar
     held lightly in my left lobe
        reminds me:
vulgar Latin *pinctor* —painter

the Tatra Mountains set before us
    like a canvas on ~~god's~~ easel
   the 'painter' steps forward to gaze
     at June snow on peaks & crags
       white lilacs and pretty-in-pink cherries
   steps back and turns – restored – towards
      Monday morning
        drudgery

2
the easel is an ass
   bearing the blank canvas
     on stout asinine legs
trudging to sublime heights
   blinkered

3
monotone days
        traipse
                uneven paths
        eyes downcast
                watching for ruts

still stumble
        slide
                sometimes fall

as the horse did that time on the way to Morskie Oko

but then vision lifts
                        scopes
                                vistas
                        balances
                on the fine rim
        of lake and
mountain

~~god's~~ compass
                &
god's eye
reiterate this landscape

Bataclan Paris

13 November - 16 November

    pebbles on a beach
    worn down by rip tide
    spill and jostle for breath

    friday the thirteenth —
    lately there is no exit
    no waking dream no
    ingenious solution
    no oneiric resolution

Bataclan Paris
organised barbarism —
paleolithic curse

' . . . gunman in the eye
he was young in his twenties
calmly reloading'

        whorled calcium shells
        dissolve into fatal white dust
        clouds of destruction

'ran to lighting room
right of stage — ten people there
there was no exit
we had run from one trap to
next — we waited for silence

'. . . reloading their guns
so we ran across the stage
saw them firing on
piles of people in the room
saw scene of carnage

'woman twice wounded
bleeding losing consciousness
carried her to exit'

others hung from
upstairs window sills — let go
hobbled down back street

'they strafed the restaurant
as one we fell to the floor
we stayed there for a minute

'I noticed a woman
next to me — she was
fatally wounded'
her reporter's voice without
any emotion

    . . . interrupt this nightmare
    to bring bodies piled three deep —
    pebbles on fraught beach

Entrevaux's mayor
checks his watch one more time
then leads whole village
through narrow streets to midday
at *Porte d'Italie*

steps into dignity
stands on war memorial
requests a minute's silence

through tears we read the
rollcall of world war one
dead for *liberté*
égalité fraternité
a century ago

in clear blue midi sky
we read the names
of Friday's victims —

on March 22nd Bruxelles terror attack

23 March 2016

there are no words left
we used them all too soon —
not knowing worse was to come.

I should have hoarded some
for this next catastrophe.
shall I say *je suis Bruxelles* —

say we are all victims now
innocent casualties and
suicide bombers both?

say: yesterday I
walked by the old port & saw
still-silver dead fish
dumped on clear seabed
dulled blank eyes questioning why?

Hag Haiku

> 25 November 2012

Once I saw her   witch
on a broomstick silhouette
against a blue moon /

Now I am that hag
I witness blood-red skies   no
innocent sunrise

Black dress black gloves black
         bra   evidence enough —
                   and a cat named 'Ashes'!

Tried to understand
         the significance of 'Bee Box' —
                   not autobiography

Now witch cat and broom
        chase hat and dragon
                while we find conkers acorns

and name Silver Birch —
        as twilight gathers
                I proffer garnered knowledge

try to understand
        significance of 'Bee Box' —
                as autobiography

Two red kite boil on high
        descry **CAPITAL LETTERS** —
                etched trunks on blank field.

Murmuration swirls
        makes pointillist *sturnus* sketch
                on a *stormus* sky

Endnotes

These poems were predominantly written during 2015. On January 1st of that year, I commenced a year-long project. The challenge I set myself: to write at least one haiku a day. I found the challenge liberated my poetic voice; each day I simply had to write 17 syllables before midnight. Some days, that's all I did; literally writing my 17 syllables at a few minutes to midnight. However, I soon found that the daily acts of attention required in order to write led to many more than 17 syllables. Often, I wrote tanka, or renga, or longer sequences composed of roughly three-line syllabic verse. The challenge forced my poetic sensibilities to be fully awake daily, and for my poetic craftsmanship to be up to the task of catching the momentary combination of perception, image, and emotion at any time of day or night. The initial result was enough material to fill several normal-sized poetry books. My gentle reader will be relieved to hear that this book is the result of a further two year's work of relentless editing, cutting and revision. The rest was written, as the poet Basil Bunting once put it, 'for the wastepaper basket'!

'Cancer Diary 1'
The quotation is from Gerald du Maurier, actor and father of Daphne du Maurier.

'Lent in Provence Vert 1'
ECITO: Europe Central Inland Transport Organisation, which was created to try and sort out the chaotic transport situation left in Europe at the end of WW2—bombed railway bridges, etc., railway engines and rolling stock far from their countries of origin, etc. My mother was PA to the Director.

'Funereal Reflections'
The historian, Tom Lloyd, thoughtfully sent an extract from the highly gothic, E. Spence. *Summer Excursions*. Volume II. 1809, after giving a detailed talk on the history and architecture of Eglwys Gymyn, half a mile from my home.

'Cancer Diary 4'
When I was 8 years old, my parents, Valerie June Dennis and Harold Noel Dennis (aka Denny) dealt with my mother's cancer by removing me from the scene. I stayed three weeks in Torquay with relatives while June had a mastectomy.

'at Dylan's Shed'
First draft written in Dylan Thomas's writing shed, looking over the same scene as that depicted in 'Poem in October'.

'Sousse Massacre'
An elderly woman from Egwys Gymyn remembered the beach at Sousse which had camels on it thirty-five years ago when she visited it.

'leaving Anywhere'
As we set off for Kraków Poland that August, the latest news about immigrants drowning was that search teams in the Mediterranean did not expect to find any more survivors from a boat carrying around 600 migrants which sank off Libya, and that more than 2,000 migrants had already died in 2015 trying to cross the Mediterranean to reach Europe.

'Light Haiku 2'
DAWN is in Lucinda Bright font.

'Hag Haiku'
CAPITAL LETTERS are in Mistral script.
sturnus Latin: starling.
stormus Welsh: stormy.